4.95
+Ca.

Take

D0637404

By
Philip J. Carter & Kenneth A. Russell

Joint editors of the
MENSA PUZZLE GROUP JOURNAL

BLANDFORD

First published in the UK 1988 by **Blandford Press**
An imprint of Cassell,
Artillery House, Artillery Row, London SW1P 1RT

Distributed in the United States by
Sterling Publishing Co., Inc.,
2 Park Avenue, New York, NY 10016

Distributed in Australia by
Capricorn Link (Australia) Pty Ltd,
PO Box 665, Lane Cove, NSW 2066

British Library Cataloguing in Publication Data

Carter, Philip J.
Take the I.Q. test.
1. Intelligence tests.
I. Title   II. Russell, Kenneth, _1928–_
153.9'3

ISBN 0-7137-2054-9

Typeset by Fakenham Photosetting Ltd, Fakenham, Norfolk

Printed in Great Britain by Cox & Wyman Ltd, Reading, Berks

Mensa Societies

UK

British Mensa Ltd.,
Bond House,
St John's Square,
Wolverhampton,
WV2 4AH.

Australia

Australian Mensa,
16 Elliot Avenue,
Carnegie,
Victoria 3163.

USA

American Mensa Ltd.,
2626 E14 Street,
Brooklyn,
N.Y. 11235.

International

Mensa International Ltd.,
15 The Ivories,
6–8 Northampton Street,
London,
N1 2HY.

Introduction

What is an 'IQ'? The letters stand for 'Intelligence Quotient'. The definition of intelligence is 'the ability to comprehend quickly' and quotient is the number of times that one number will divide into another. Thus a child of eight years of age who successfully passed a test for a child of ten years of age would have an 'IQ' of ten divided by eight = $1.25 \times 100 = 125$. A child of eight years of age who successfully passed a test for a child of eight, but failed a test for a child of nine years would have an 'IQ' of eight divided by eight = $1 \times 100 = 100$, which would be the norm.

With adults this method of calculation would not apply. They would be judged on an 'IQ' test where the average score would be 100 and the results would be graded above and below this norm accordingly to known test scores.

It is generally agreed that intelligence is inherited and that 50 per cent of the population would have an 'IQ' of between 90 per cent and 110 per cent. Approximately 25 per cent would be above and 25 per cent below this mark. Above this central group about 14.5 per cent of the population would have 'IQ's of 110 to 120; 7 per cent would have 'IQ's of 120 to 130; and 3.5 per cent would have 'IQ's of 130 or above. Below the central group we find 14.5 per cent having 'IQ's between 80 and 90; 7 per cent between 70 and 80 and the remaining 3.5 per cent below 70.

Intelligence tests only measure one's ability to reason, they do not measure the other qualities which are required for success, such as character, personality, talent, persistence and application, etc.

A person with a high 'IQ' has a much better chance of success in life than a person with a low 'IQ' but only if that person applies him or herself to the tasks ahead diligently and with enthusiasm. Someone with a relatively low 'IQ' but with a high sense of achievement and great persistence can fare better in life than a bright person.

About the Authors

Kenneth A. Russell is a London surveyor and is also the Puzzle Editor of Mensa, the high I.Q. Society.

Philip J. Carter is an engineering estimator and also a Yorkshire J.P. He is editor of *Enigmasig*, the journal of the Mensa Special Interest Puzzle Group.

Acknowledgements

The authors are greatly indebted to their wives, both named Barbara, who, as well as supporting them enthusiastically in writing the book, have also contributed in compiling, checking and typing the manuscript.

Appreciation is also given to Victor Serebriakoff, Mensa's Honorary President, for his encouragement on our various projects and to the Mensa Committee for allowing the use of the name Mensa on the front cover of this book.

Instructions

There are four complete tests numbered One, Two, Three and Four.

Each test has ten parts numbered with Roman numerals.

You have limited time so keep strictly to the time limit. Any delay could invalidate your score, so work as quickly as possible.

Don't spend too much time on any one question; if in doubt leave it and return to it using the time remaining. If you do not know an answer, have an intuitive guess; this may well be the correct answer!

Note: Dots indicate the number of letters in a missing word, i.e. (. . . .) means that there are four letters in the word.

TEST ONE

Part I is a series of twenty questions designed to test your ability in collecting together objects or ideas which belong to a set, or have some common attribute. To make this classification simpler we have put together a series of words and you have to spot the 'odd one out'. There are five words and only four of them have a common theme; underline the '<u>odd one</u>'.

You have ten minutes to complete the twenty questions.

Classification

Example: bag, basket, <u>hat</u>, pocket, bucket

Answer: <u>hat</u>; the other four are used for carrying things.

1. globe, orb, sphere, sceptre, ball
2. horde, mob, rush, throng, host
3. irons, scissors, chains, fetters, shackles
4. abode, dwelling, house, residence, street
5. inquiry, exploration, investigation, deliberation, probe
6. triad, triune, trilby, tripod, trine
7. abridge, conclude, decrease, curtail, abbreviate
8. flutter, air, soar, wing, hover
9. hail, enter, address, salute, welcome
10. commotion, sound, bedlam, din, furore
11. aroma, odour, fragrance, redolence, repugnance
12. scold, scoff, deride, jeer, mock
13. honour, credit, esteem, judge, accolade
14. record, standard, bench-mark, model, example
15. broker, middleman, businessman, distributor, intermediary
16. dais, rostrum, arena, stage, podium
17. howl, ululate, bewail, grieve, lament
18. apparition, illusion, hallucination, illustration, phantasm
19. mountain, zenith, apex, summit, peak
20. sector, area, region, district, land

 8–10   AVERAGE
11–13   GOOD
14–16   VERY GOOD
17–20   EXCEPTIONAL

Each correct answer scores one point

Part II is a series of twenty questions designed to test your knowledge of language and your ability to spot words which have the same meaning. We have grouped together five words and from them you have to underline the word which means the same or has the closest meaning to the KEY word.

You have ten minutes to complete the twenty questions.

Synonyms

Example: ANGULAR (blunt, stiff, abrupt, <u>branching</u>,
      cornered)

Answer: <u>branching</u> is the word closest in meaning to the KEY
      word, ANGULAR.

1. EXCUSE (blame, reject, mediate, condone, resolve)
2. AVERAGE (poor, mean, public, weak, value)
3. SOURCE (trace, culmination, report, read, origin)
4. ROSTER (index, place, register, stage, election)
5. INCREASE (profit, amplify, size, mitigate, moderate)
6. EASY (elementary, artful, infantile, pretentious, well)
7. SLUMP (sleep, crash, recline, bend, kneel)
8. SUNDRY (assorted, always, plentiful, many, all)
9. HEARSAY (evidence, rumour, lies, sound, investigation)
10. CONFRONT (amaze, abash, tally, verify, face)
11. COMPLETE (formulate, absolute, change, ending, stop)
12. MELLOW (deep, ripe, strange, shallow, backward)
13. SALLOW (dark, unmanly, narrow, wan, bloated)
14. RECREANT (craven, disagreeable, unrelaxed,
    indulgent, violent)
15. INDOMITABLE (evident, steadfast, veritable, defeatist,
    calm)
16. PANACHE (humour, flair, strain, movement, manner)
17. CULVERT (road, drain, track, river, ditch)
18. TORPID (sluggish, warlike, gushing, argumentative,
    old)
19. SEER (magician, prophet, professor, noble, artist)
20. PSEUDO (extra, bogus, close, true, special)

8–10	AVERAGE	14–16	VERY GOOD
11–13	GOOD	17–20	EXCEPTIONAL

Each correct answer scores one point

Part III is a series of twenty questions designed to test your knowledge of language and your ability to visualise opposite meanings quickly. We have grouped together five words and from them you have to underline the <u>word</u> which means the opposite or is as nearly as possible opposite in meaning to the KEY word.

You have ten minutes to complete the twenty questions.

Antonyms

Example: CARELESS (exact, <u>heedful</u>, strict, anxious, dutiful)

Answer: <u>heedful</u> is the word which means the opposite of the KEY word CARELESS.

1. PRECARIOUS (easy, carefree, safe, harmless, cautious)
2. CIVIL (political, military, urbane, war, battle)
3. GAIN (depart, destroy, retain, lose, earn)
4. SIMPLE (artistic, intricate, long, tortuous, busy)
5. FEEBLE (strength, mighty, well, robust, adequate)
6. THRIFT (waste, invest, economy, spend, purchase)
7. HIDEOUS (normal, generous, handsome, fair, logical)
8. FRESH (raw, late, asleep, weary, rest)
9. EXONERATE (imprison, accuse, tax, complain, expel)
10. SOOTH (mollify, savage, excite, amaze, transform)
11. PREJUDICE (judge, impartiality, change, bias, concern)
12. ROUGH (courteous, regular, etiquette, harmonic, estimate)
13. OBSCURE (deep, recondite, evident, answer, truth)
14. CULTURE (vanity, taste, vulgarity, sloth, envy)
15. DISAVOW (pray, permit, challenge, claim, gather)
16. TART (tasty, sweet, cake, strong, blunt)
17. LOYAL (unofficial, apathetic, carefree, uncivil, rebellious)
18. VINDICATE (excuse, condemn, imprison, defend, summons)
19. NECESSARY (inadvertent, needless, poverty, rejected, dismissed)
20. MEEK (haughty, controlled, irate, introvert, loud)

| 8–10 | AVERAGE | 14–16 | VERY GOOD |
| 11–13 | GOOD | 17–20 | EXCEPTIONAL |

Each correct answer scores one point

Part IV is a series of twenty questions designed to test your ability to visualise relationships between various objects and ideas. We have grouped together five words, one of which will pair up with the KEY word to produce a similar relationship to the two-word example. Underline the <u>word</u> which is appropriate.

You have ten minutes to complete the twenty questions.

Analogy

Example: TIRED is to work as
HAPPY is to (sleep, rest, <u>success</u>, exercise, eating)

Answer: <u>success</u> has a similar relationship to HAPPY as work has to TIRED.

1. OASIS   is to sand as
   ISLAND   is to (sea, river, water, waves, pond)

2. CASTLE   is to defence as
   THEATRE   is to (audience, play, arena, entertainment, vaudeville)

3. PLUM   is to fruit as
   WILLOW   is to (wood, tree, evergreen, leaves, branch)

4. CHAPTER   is to book as
   ACT   is to (stage, read, perform, play, award)

5. SWERVE   is to veer as
   ROTATE   is to (fluctuate, sway, gyrate, surge, deviate)

6. CASINO   is to gambling as
      MOSQUE   is to (church, **worship**, Muslim, orient, God)

7. ROUGH   is to polished as
      RUDE   is to (**refined**, royal, shapeless, clever, fair)

8. HELMET   is to protection as
      TIARA   is to (**adornment**, queen, hair, royalty, head)

9. SINGLE   is to one as
      CIPHER   is to (hundred, ten, five, two, **zero**)

10. CATAPULT   is to fling as
       RIFLE   is to (gun, bullet, trigger, **fire**, army)

11. FOX   is to fur as
       PEACOCK   is to (tail, **plumage**, fly, claws, beak)

12. PATROL   is to security as
       INSURANCE   is to (finance, selling, **protection**, policy, money)

13. HEED   is to neglect as
       PACIFY   is to (war, victory, allay, **incite**, refuse)

14. INSTITUTE   is to academy as
       DECREE   is to (**mandate**, marriage, judge, court, blame)

15. LACE   is to fabric as
       MUTTON   is to (sheep, stew, **meat**, animal, food)

16. LIP   is to mouth as
       HEM   is to (sewing, cloth, **fringe**, fold, trim)

17. EVENING   is to night as
       AUTUMN   is to (summer, season, spring, day, **winter**)

18. IMPRISON   is to jail as
       EXILE   is to (punishment, **banish**, country, depart, sea)

19. KNIFE   is to cut as
       AXE   is to (sever, lacerate, **chop**, slice, impale)

20. FAWN   is to deer as
     HEIFER   is to (animal, sheep, elephant, pig, cow)

 8–10 AVERAGE
11–13 GOOD
14–16 VERY GOOD
17–20 EXCEPTIONAL

Each correct answer scores one point

TEST ONE • PART V

Part V is a series of twenty questions designed to test your knowledge of language and your ability to quickly recognise words of similar meanings. There are six words in each question and you have to find a pair of words which have similar meanings. Underline the <u>two words</u> which you believe to be closest in meaning.

You have ten minutes to complete the twenty questions.

Synonyms II

Example: <u>walk</u>, run, drive, <u>stroll</u>, fly, sit

Answer: <u>walk</u> and <u>stroll</u> are the two words in the list which are closest in meaning.

1. solve, curious, inquire, advance, reason, probe
2. circus, ceremony, award, pageant, splendour, vanity
3. mere, crucial, sheer, basic, capacity, essential
4. generous, bequest, legacy, endow, expert, award
5. grumble, fluster, sob, tear, sorrow, wail
6. shock, débâcle, onrush, error, demise, fiasco
7. flap, pivot, dash, flick, spin, stir
8. weather, rain, humid, cloud, moist, torrid
9. dust, mar, concrete, paint, soil, consecrate
10. tall, degree, diet, lean, slender, shape
11. principal, first, before, initial, direct, élite
12. docile, manage, able, submissive, fair, true
13. smirk, laugh, shout, cough, leer, snarl
14. parody, comedy, laugh, satire, wisecrack, event
15. occupation, resolve, vocation, allegory, temper, earn
16. sing, grunt, sound, talk, whistle, chatter
17. merge, thread, hammer, smelt, force, wrinkle
18. misfit, eccentric, vile, spare, insulting, irregular
19. calf, sow, cat, hog, pup, foal
20. elder, better, bulk, teacher, friend, senior

8–10   AVERAGE
11–13   GOOD
14–16   VERY GOOD
17–20   EXCEPTIONAL

Each correct answer scores one point

TEST ONE • PART VI

Part VI is a series of twenty questions designed to test your knowledge of language and your ability to quickly recognise words of opposite meaning. There are six words in each question and you have to find a pair of words which have opposite meanings. Underline the <u>two words</u> which you believe to be opposite in meaning.

You have ten minutes to complete the twenty questions.

Antonyms II

Example: curved, long, <u>big</u>, <u>small</u>, broad, fat

Answer: <u>big</u> and <u>small</u> are the two words in the list which are opposite in meaning.

1. marriage, cohabitation, part, separation, fraternise, divorce
2. dark, true, slander, false, accuse, test
3. joy, passion, rage, emotion, fear, calm
4. faint, weak, large, sturdy, great, serious
5. speech, coarse, manners, argue, file, cultured
6. sickly, exceptional, strong, divisive, ordinary, unwell
7. proceed, permit, evermore, forbid, attempt, concede
8. remit, rent, spend, share, hoard, money
9. observe, clear, distance, thick, horizon, obscure
10. buy, barter, estimate, sell, find, trade
11. unique, straight, product, usual, peculiar, spatial
12. relate, advise, write, know, deceive, impart
13. asleep, unruffled, smart, cold, jumpy, unconscious
14. theft, hope, veracity, feelings, joy, dishonesty
15. well, exquisite, cheap, pale, old, nasty
16. sweetness, flashy, cunning, rancour, tasty, regret
17. sly, steadfast, regular, irresolute, pitiful, sorrowful
18. care, punish, seek, ask, consider, disregard
19. frugality, essence, goods, extravagance, nonsense, purchase
20. befriend, charm, allay, position, tempt, rouse

8–10	AVERAGE	14–16	VERY GOOD
11–13	GOOD	17–20	EXCEPTIONAL

Each correct answer scores one point

TEST ONE • PART VII

Part VII is a series of twenty questions designed to test your ability to quickly find alternative meanings of words. You are looking for a word which has the same meaning as one word or phrase in one sense, and the same meaning as a different word or phrase in another sense. The dots represent the number of letters in the missing word. Fill in the missing word.

You have twenty minutes to complete the twenty questions.

Double Meanings

Example: breathes heavily . . . . . underclothes

Answer: pants.

1. financial institution . . . side of river

2. body of water . . . combined stakes

3. abstain . . . . . . chorus of a song

4. tool for boring holes . . . . . rigorous exercises

5. financial penalty . . . very good of its kind

6. official position . . . . highly offensive

7. give account of . . . . . . noise from a gun

8. emerge from egg . . . . . lower half of divided door

9. deputy head of monastery . . . . . previous

10. move from side to side . . . . large mass of stone

11. first in importance . . . . . prepare

12. rub hard . . . . . arid land containing stunted vegetation

13. compartment in a stable . . . . . employ delaying tactics

14. conceal . . . . skin of an animal

15. incline . . . . not fat

16. intermediate . . . . miserly

17. evergreen coniferous tree . . . . yearn

18. apparatus for weaving yarn . . . . come into view

19. feed on grass, pasture . . . . . scrape

20. large bag . . . . to plunder

8–10 AVERAGE
11–13 GOOD
14–16 VERY GOOD
17–20 EXCEPTIONAL

Each correct answer scores one point

Part VIII is a series of twenty questions designed to test your ability at innovation. You are given the first part of the word or phrase, and you have to find the second part. The same second part then becomes the first part of a second word or phrase. The dots represent the number of letters in the missing word. Fill in the missing word.

You have twenty minutes to complete the twenty questions.

Double-words

Example: house . . . . all

Answer: hold.

1. ring . . . . . . stroke

2. double . . . . . reference

3. left . . . react

4. hard . . . bone

5. door . . . child

6. news . . . . weight

7. screen . . . thing

8. skin . . . . seated

9. mean . . . . piece

10. trade . . . . up

11. push . . . . . man

12. check . . . . . blank

13. post . . . . line

14. third . . . . payer

15. ever . . . . . keeper

16. knee . . . . freeze

17. heart . . . . . down

18. closed . . . . breaker

19. dust . . . . wheel

20. back . . . . . work

8–10 AVERAGE
11–13 GOOD
14–16 VERY GOOD
17–20 EXCEPTIONAL

Each correct answer scores one point

Part IX is a series of ten culture-free tests designed to test your powers of logical reasoning, and understanding of relationships, pattern and design. Study each display of diagrams and select the missing item from the choices given. Study the instructions given to each question.

You have twenty minutes to complete the ten questions.

Example: Ƨ   is to   / / / /

    as   0   is to   ⊬ , /// , ∞ , =

Answer: =   has the same relationship to   0

    as   / / / /   has to   Ƨ .

1.

    is to   +

as

is to:

A	B	C	D	E	F

2.

Which of the five boxes below
is most like the box on the left?

A   B   C   D   E

3.

Which of the five boxes below
is most like the box on the left?

A   B   C   D   E

4.

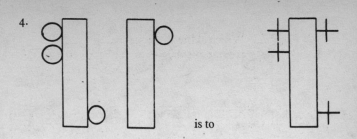

is to

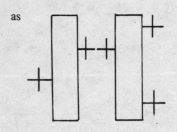

as

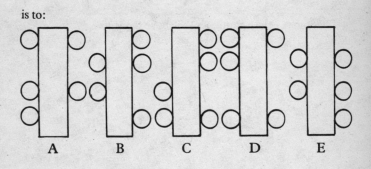

is to:

A   B   C   D   E

5.

Which of the following continues the above sequence?

A B C D E

6.

What figure below continues the above sequence?

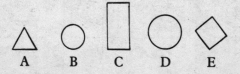

A B C D E

7. Study the array of tiles below and select the one that you think logically is the missing tile from the choice given.

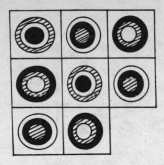

Choose from:

A   B   C   D

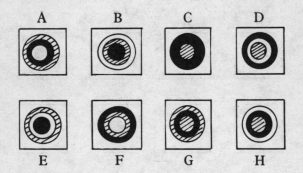

E   F   G   H

8. Look along each line horizontally and down each line vertically and decide from the choice given what you think should logically be the missing tile.

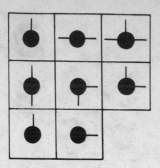

Choose from:

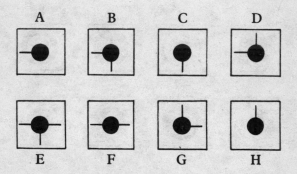

A   B   C   D

E   F   G   H

28

9.

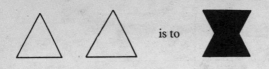 is to

as

is to:

A   B   C   D   E

10.

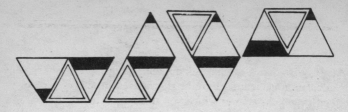

Which figure below continues the above sequence?

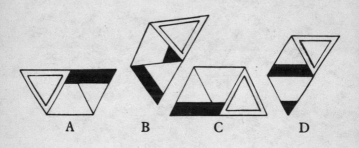

A   B   C   D

8–10   AVERAGE
12–14   GOOD
16   VERY GOOD
18–20   EXCEPTIONAL

Each correct answer scores two points

TEST ONE • PART X

Part X is a series of ten tests designed to test your powers of calculation and logic. From the alternatives given in each question choose the answer which you think is correct.

You have twenty minutes to solve the ten questions.

Example: My watch shows the time at 12.25; one clock shows
12.10. The radio announces 12.30, the church clock
strikes 12.00, and your watch shows 12.15. The
correct time is 12.20. What is the average time, fast
or slow, as shown by these time-pieces?

A.	2 min slow	B.	4 min slow	C.	6 min slow
D.	2 min fast	E.	4 min fast	F.	6 min fast

Answer: B.   4 min slow.

1.   Alan is older than Bill and Colin. Colin is older than
Dave. Edward is younger than Bill but older than Dave.
Edward is younger than Colin. Alan is younger than Fred.
Who is the oldest man?

A.	Alan	B.	Bill	C.	Colin
D.	Dave	E.	Edward	F.	Fred

2.   A company asks its workforce to increase production by 4
per cent per week. If the company worked a six-day week,
how much would they need to produce per day extra to
achieve the desired 4 per cent weekly increase?

A.	0.666 per cent	B.	1.2 per cent	C.	1.5 per cent
D.	3 per cent	E.	4 per cent	F.	6 per cent

3.   Jim has £3 more than Sid, but if Sid had three times more
than he has now, he would have £3 more than the
combined original amounts of money. How much money
has Jim?

A.	£4	B.	£5	C.	£6
D.	£7	E.	£9	F.	£11

4. A car travels 20 miles in the same time as another car, travelling 20 m.p.h. faster, covers 30 miles. How long does the journey take?

A.	28 min	B.	29 min	C.	30 min
D.	31 min	E.	31.5 min	F.	32.5 min

5. From London to Coventry a motorist knows three different routes, from Coventry to Leeds he knows six different routes and from Leeds to Newcastle he knows two different routes. How many routes does he know from London to Newcastle?

A.	11	B.	18	C.	27
D.	36	E.	38	F.	45

6. On glancing through your morning paper you notice that four pages are missing. One of the missing pages is 21. The back page of the newspaper is 28. What are the numbers of the other three missing pages?

A.	6, 7, 20	B.	7, 8, 20	C.	7, 8, 22
D.	8, 9, 22	E.	9, 10, 22	F.	10, 11, 22

7. A batsman is out for 23 runs, which raises his batting average for the season from 15 to 16. How many runs would he have to score to bring his average up to 18?

A.	27	B.	33	C.	37
D.	39	E.	42	F.	48

8. A piece of wire 32 in long is cut into two strips, each of which is bent to form a perfect square. The sum of the areas of the two squares is 34 sq.in. What are the lengths of the two pieces of wire?

A.	9 in and 23 in	B.	8 in and 24 in
C.	12 in and 20 in	D.	14 in and 16 in
E.	15 in and 17 in	F.	16 in and 16 in

9. Imagine two bags. Each bag contains eight counters, four red and four yellow. A counter is drawn out of bag one and another counter out of bag two. What are the chances that at least one of the counters will be yellow?

    A. 1 in 4   B. 1 in 3   C. 1 in 2
    D. 2 in 3   E. 3 in 4   F. Certainty

10. A man drives to a certain destination 24 miles away at a speed of 48 m.p.h. and arrives in 30 min. On his return journey, however, he decides to slow down and his identical return journey takes him 60 min. What is his average speed for the total round trip?

    A. 30 m.p.h.   B. 32 m.p.h.   C. 36 m.p.h.
    D. 38 m.p.h.   E. 40 m.p.h.   F. 42 m.p.h.

8–10	AVERAGE
12–14	GOOD
16	VERY GOOD
18–20	EXCEPTIONAL

Each correct answer scores two points

TEST ONE • PART I
1. sceptre 2. rush 3. scissors 4. street 5. deliberation
6. trilby 7. conclude 8. air 9. enter 10. sound
11. repugnance 12. scold 13. judge 14. record
15. businessman 16. arena 17. grieve 18. illustration
19. mountain 20. land

TEST ONE • PART II
1. condone 2. mean 3. origin 4. register 5. amplify
6. elementary 7. crash 8. assorted 9. rumour 10. face
11. absolute 12. ripe 13. wan 14. craven 15. steadfast
16. flair 17. drain 18. sluggish 19. prophet 20. bogus

TEST ONE • PART III
1. safe 2. military 3. lose 4. intricate 5. robust
6. waste 7. handsome 8. weary 9. accuse 10. excite
11. impartiality 12. courteous 13. evident 14. vulgarity
15. permit 16. sweet 17. rebellious 18. condemn
19. needless 20. haughty

TEST ONE • PART IV
1. water 2. entertainment 3. tree 4. play 5. gyrate
6. worship 7. refined 8. adornment 9. zero 10. fire
11. plumage 12. protection 13. incite 14. mandate
15. meat 16. cloth 17. winter 18. banish 19. chop
20. cow

TEST ONE • PART V
1. inquire, probe 2. ceremony, pageant 3. crucial,
essential 4. bequest, legacy 5. sob, wail 6. débâcle,
fiasco 7. pivot, spin 8. humid, moist 9. mar,
soil 10. lean, slender 11. first, initial 12. docile,
submissive 13. smirk, leer 14. parody,
satire 15. occupation, vocation 16. talk,

chatter 17. merge, smelt 18. eccentric,
irregular 19. sow, hog 20. elder, senior

TEST ONE ● PART VI
1. marriage, divorce 2. true, false 3. rage,
calm 4. weak, sturdy 5. coarse, cultured 6. exceptional,
ordinary 7. permit, forbid 8. spend, hoard 9. clear,
obscure 10. buy, sell 11. unique, usual 12. advise,
deceive 13. unruffled, jumpy 14. veracity,
dishonesty 15. exquisite, nasty 16. sweetness,
rancour 17. steadfast, irresolute 18. consider,
disregard 19. frugality, extravagance 20. allay, rouse

TEST ONE ● PART VII
1. bank 2. pool 3. refrain 4. drill 5. fine 6. rank
7. report 8. hatch 9. prior 10. rock 11. prime
12. scrub 13. stall 14. hide 15. lean 16. mean
17. pine 18. loom 19. graze 20. sack

TEST ONE ● PART VIII
1. master 2. cross 3. over 4. back 5. step 6. paper
7. play 8. deep 9. time 10. mark 11. chair
12. point 13. date 14. rate 15. green 16. deep
17. break 18. circuit 19. cart 20. ground

TEST ONE ● PART IX
1. B   6. A.
2. E   7. E.
3. D   8. G.
4. B   9. C.
5. C   10. D.

TEST ONE ● PART X
1. F. Fred   6. C. 7, 8, 22
2. E. 4 per cent   7. D. 39
3. E. £9   8. C. 12 in and 20 in
4. C. 30 min   9. E. 3 in 4
5. D. 36   10. B. 32 m.p.h.

TOTAL SCORE

80–100	AVERAGE
101–130	GOOD
131–160	VERY GOOD
161–200	EXCEPTIONAL

TEST TWO

TEST TWO • PART I

Part I is a series of twenty questions designed to test your ability in collecting together objects or ideas which belong to a set, or have some common attribute. To make this classification simpler we have put together a series of words and you have to spot the 'odd one out'. There are five words and only four of them have a common theme; underline the 'odd one'.

You have ten minutes to complete the twenty questions.

Classification

Example: bag, basket, <u>hat</u>, pocket, bucket

Answer: <u>hat</u>, the other four are used for carrying things.

1. cavity, angle, bend, joint, corner
2. filibuster, marine, freebooter, pirate, buccaneer
3. badger, harass, harry, strike, annoy
4. spot, ink, blemish, blot, stain
5. cage, fold, hutch, sty, cell
6. slouch, fail, droop, loll, slump
7. coming, hereafter, subsequent, future, arrival
8. size, manikin, gnome, homuncule, pygmy
9. alp, fell, peak, dale, mount
10. burglar, arsonist, embezzler, bandit, purloiner
11. agenda, index, timetable, programme, schedule
12. trend, vogue, fashion, dress, mode
13. intrepid, rash, confident, dauntless, fearless
14. rave, yell, argue, rant, vociferate
15. revolt, mutiny, insubordination, challenge, rebellion.
16. cobalt, cyan, verdant, azure, navy
17. core, centre, heart, medium, hub
18. mature, ripe, adult, virile, developed
19. intern, detain, parole, confine, constrain
20. slash, sever, cut, snick, lacerate

  8–10   AVERAGE
11–13   GOOD
14–16   VERY GOOD
17–20   EXCEPTIONAL

Each correct answer scores one point

Part II is a series of twenty questions designed to test your knowledge of language and your ability to spot words which have the same meaning. We have grouped together five words and from them you have to underline the <u>word</u> which means the same or has the closest meaning to the KEY word.

You have ten minutes to complete the twenty questions.

Synonyms

Example: ANGULAR (blunt, stiff, abrupt, <u>branching</u>, cornered)

Answer: <u>branching</u> is the word closest in meaning to the KEY word, ANGULAR.

1. SECURE (comfortable, home, found, escorted, secret)
2. INDISCREET (guarded, prudent, random, rash, mixed)
3. AUTHENTIC (duplicate, adept, factual, reasonable, similar)
4. STABLE (transitory, equine, vacillating, resolute, boring)
5. MUTUAL (separate, common, agreement, distrust, active)
6. SOLACE (alone, mistake, friendship, comfort, misery)
7. SWEET (plush, song, dulcet, rhythm, taste)
8. NAUSEA (obscenity, anger, fright, love, sickness)
9. PRINCIPAL (axiom, chief, rule, interest, obligation)
10. STAID (old, just, unsteady, sedate, false)

11. ROOT (branch, perch, plant, seed, base)
12. HESITANT (resolute, thinking, reluctant, considerate, paltry)
13. PALPABLE (obvious, joyous, pulsating, easy, strange)
14. MOGUL (tyrant, tycoon, terror, prince, soldier)
15. EPITHET (letter, passage, description, name, note)
16. PARAMETER (boundary, meaning, specification, law, pattern)
17. ALLEGORY (story, dislike, message, claim, passage)
18. TENDER (gift, accept, incline, offer, resign)
19. TENABLE (false, viable, inviting, changeable, doubtful)
20. TRESS (mane, hair, poach, ropeway, braid)

8–10 AVERAGE
11–13 GOOD
14–16 VERY GOOD
17–20 EXCEPTIONAL

Each correct answer scores one point

Part III is a series of twenty questions designed to test your knowledge of language and your ability to visualise opposite meanings quickly. We have grouped together five words and from them you have to underline the <u>word</u> which means the opposite or is as nearly as possible opposite in meaning to the KEY word.

You have ten minutes to complete the twenty questions.

Antonyms

Example: CARELESS (exact, <u>heedful</u>, strict, anxious, dutiful)

Answer: <u>heedful</u> is the word which means the opposite of the
KEY word CARELESS.

1. HEIGHT (decline, slope, width, depression, basement)
2. CRUEL (painless, effortless, happy, quick, gentle)
3. LEGAL (wrong, illicit, trespass, base, convict)
4. REDUCE (enhance, cultivate, deepen, raise, obtain)
5. SERIOUS (giddy, mistaken, untrustworthy, stupid, careless)
6. EXPOSE (divulge, dress, cloak, furbish, clean)
7. REFUSE (arrive, appear, waste, greet, receive)
8. SPECIAL (cheap, old, common, peculiar, rare)
9. ORDER (freedom, destroy, mob, chaos, rite)
10. TIE (link, loosen, different, precarious, knot)
11. REAL (spurious, constructed, found, bad, story)
12. UNHEALTHY (nourished, salubrious, cultivated, obvious, fine)

13. SANCTIFY (**dedicate**, release, pollute, privatise, **venerate**)
14. PIETY (sloppiness, wickedness, loneliness, **devotion**, division)
15. PUNISH (release, commend, **correct**, deter, **chastise**)
16. SLENDER (adequate, tall, moderate, great, **stout**)
17. CONTENT (**angry**, querulous, fawning, proficient, unclear)
18. ZEAL (weakness, failure, piquancy, **apathy**, slow)
19. PRODIGAL (**prudent**, profuse, gifted, related, pointed)
20. MANIFEST (**show**, dim, black, note, doubtful)

8–10 AVERAGE
11–13 GOOD
14–16 VERY GOOD
17–20 EXCEPTIONAL

Each correct answer scores one point

Part IV is a series of twenty questions designed to test your ability to visualise relationships between various objects and ideas. We have grouped together five words, one of which will pair up with the KEY word to produce a similar relationship to the two-word example. Underline the <u>word</u> which is appropriate.

You have ten minutes to complete the twenty questions.

Analogy

Example: TIRED is to work as
HAPPY is to (sleep, rest, <u>success</u>, exercise, eating)

Answer: <u>success</u> has a similar relationship to HAPPY as work has to TIRED.

1. ARTIST is to paint as
   TAILOR is to (trousers, suit, fashion, cloth, scissors)

2. TASTE is to tongue as
   WALK is to (pavement, toes, field, legs, ankles)

3. MILK is to liquid as
   ANGER is to (fear, emotion, noise, temper, stress)

4. PLENTY is to enough as
   RUDE is to (imp, quick, churlish, bad, pitiful)

5. DEBRIS is to buildings as
   FRAGMENTS is to (powder, delicate, carpet, vase, scrap)

6. PINT   is to capacity as
    OUNCE   is to (pound, weight, amount, portion, unit)

7. HONEST   is to false as
    OFFEND   is to (insult, present, give, please, serve)

8. RABBIT   is to mammal as
    BEAVER   is to (animal, amphibian, creature, rodent, dog)

9. CLAMOUR   is to noise as
    SILENCE   is to (armistice, accord, still, hush, mild)

10. HELP   is to frustrate as
    REMAIN   is to (tarry, divide, offer, withdraw, increase)

11. FRATRICIDE   is to brother as
    PATRICIDE   is to (uncle, sister, mother, mother-in-law, father)

12. RASH   is to wary as
    SINCERE   is to (thanks, false, crime, dangerous, troublesome)

13. LARGO   is to slow as
    DIMINUENDO   is to (decrease, stop, quiet, loud, fast)

14. TURMOIL   is to trouble as
    TRAGEDY   is to (sombre, disaster, pity, drama, earthquake)

15. RED   is to scarlet as
    BLUE   is to (colour, black, verdant, cyan, callow)

16. CHEMISTRY   is to substances as
    FAUNA   is to (plants, animals, reactions, soil, rocks)

17. RABIES   is to dogs as
    RINDERPEST   is to (cats, crops, grass, sheep, cattle)

18. CHANNEL   is to water as
     ISTHMUS   is to (sea, mountains, air, passage, land)

19. ITINERARY   is to journey as
     AGENDA   is to (boardroom, secretary, meeting, programme, minutes)

20. GUILD   is to association as
     FLEET   is to (ship, water, vessel, armada, sailor)

8–10   AVERAGE
11–13 GOOD
14–16 VERY GOOD
17–20 EXCEPTIONAL

Each correct answer scores one point

TEST TWO • PART V

━━━━━━━━━━━━━━━━━━━━━━━━━━━━━━━━━━

Part V is a series of twenty questions designed to test your knowledge of language and your ability to quickly recognise words of similar meanings. There are six words in each question and you have to find a pair of words which have similar meanings. Underline the <u>two words</u> which you believe to be closest in meaning.

You have ten minutes to complete the twenty questions.

Synonyms II

Example: <u>walk</u>, run, drive, <u>stroll</u>, fly, sit

Answer: <u>walk</u> and <u>stroll</u> are the two words in the list which are closest in meaning.

1. train, dispute, hunt, doubt, rouse, compose
2. spin, mild, mercy, trap, serene, distressing
3. mount, dale, bank, stream, peak, range
4. terror, scare, disgust, bell, clown, alarm
5. lively, folly, happy, bouncy, frilly, homely
6. sensual, pornographic, oppressive, erotic, naked, libido
7. travel, remote, distance, highway, absent, far
8. drizzle, frost, sun, wind, deluge, fog
9. angry, tense, free, complete, strained, emotion
10. crush, powder, saw, drill, grind, build
11. evasion, elation, event, glee, anger, serenity
12. assign, build, designate, cut, paper, phrase
13. deposit, sign, draw, invitation, indication, find
14. conserve, retreat, lose, haven, grace, garden
15. poltergeist, apparition, exorcism, terror, monster, phantom
16. doodle, write, copy, scrawl, compose, scroll
17. tailor, costume, hat, parade, arm, regalia
18. abound, myriad, march, corporation, congregate, multitude
19. urgent, bonus, staid, dead, sober, ill
20. give, adore, charm, immortalise, liaise, cherish

8–10	AVERAGE
11–13	GOOD
14–16	VERY GOOD
17–20	EXCEPTIONAL

Each correct answer scores one point

TEST TWO • PART VI

Part VI is a series of twenty questions designed to test your knowledge of language and your ability to quickly recognise words of opposite meaning. There are six words in each question and you have to find a pair of words which have opposite meanings. Underline the <u>two words</u> which you believe to be opposite in meaning.

You have ten minutes to complete the twenty questions.

Antonyms II

Example: curved, long, big, small, broad, fat

Answer: big and small are the two words in the list which are opposite in meaning.

1. weird, loose, wise, wild, dangerous, absurd
2. reply, resign, receive, employ, stay, resist
3. hungry, manly, portly, extreme, puny, diminutive
4. decorate, improve, alter, upkeep, raise, maintain
5. disperse, change, parade, assemble, convert, summons
6. cheap, honest, fair, wholesome, clever, false
7. funny, odd, condescending, charming, dejected, happy
8. destroy, mislay, seek, find, obtain, acquire
9. mourn, intern, sing, laugh, rejoice, happiness
10. fresh, noble, strong, humble, poor, peer
11. compassion, conciliation, triumph, ruthlessness, calmness, beauty
12. fracture, operation, union, colleague, continue, cut
13. thick, slow, vivid, rain, dull, ordinary
14. patient, waiting, restive, naked, morbid, quiet
15. sinful, destitute, penitent, wrong, suspended, unrepentant
16. facetious, pleasant, serious, calm, unkind, auspicious
17. continue, conclude, perform, after, intervene, introduce
18. find, alternate, append, change, replace, remove
19. defamation, joy, praise, characterise, remunerate, hope
20. allow, resent, achieve, abstain, impart, condone

8–10   AVERAGE
11–13   GOOD
14–16   VERY GOOD
17–20   EXCEPTIONAL

Each correct answer scores one point

TEST TWO • PART VII

Part VII is a series of twenty questions designed to test your ability to quickly find alternative meanings of words. You are looking for a word which has the same meaning as one word or phrase in one sense, and the same meaning as a different word or phrase in another sense. The dots represent the number of letters in the missing word. Fill in the missing word.

You have twenty minutes to complete the twenty questions.

Double Meanings

Example: breathes heavily . . . . . underclothes

Answer: pants.

1. growl viciously . . . . . tangled mass of thread, hair

2. fall behind . . . cover a cylinder

3. thin branch . . . . . fasten with adhesive substance

4. uncommon . . . . undercooked

5. device for weighing . . . . . climb to the top

6. tool for stamping . . . . . mixed drink (sometimes hot)

7. model of foot from which shoes are made . . . . continue

8. horrify . . . . . mass of hair

9. security for reappearance in court . . . . empty out water

10. sudden upturn in commercial activity . . . barrier across harbour

11. wading bird . . . . . machine for moving heavy weights

12. set of related notes . . . small island

13. balance on . . . . . measure of five yards and a half

14. place for worship . . . . . . part of the head

15. confess . . . . . allow to enter

16. evidence offered in court to support a claim . . . . container

17. securely in position . . . . a commercial enterprise

18. put through a coarse sieve . . . . . . a puzzling thing

19. firearm . . . . . search and steal

20. seductive woman . . . improvised accompaniment

  8–10   AVERAGE
11–13   GOOD
14–16   VERY GOOD
17–20   EXCEPTIONAL

Each correct answer scores one point

Part VIII is a series of twenty questions designed to test your ability at innovation. You are given the first part of the word or phrase, and you have to find the second part. The same second part then becomes the first part of a second word or phrase. The dots represent the number of letters in the missing word. Fill in the missing word.

You have twenty minutes to complete the twenty questions.

Double Words

Example: house . . . . all

Answer: hold.

1. one . . . lay

2. rear . . . . . house

3. oil . . . . head

4. slip . . . . . . lined

5. home . . . up

6. long . . . . . finder

7. shoe . . . . rate

8. drum . . . . . up

9. moor . . . . scape

10. dry . . . . . mason

11. post . . . . board

12. draw . . . . date

13. turn . . . . . spoon

14. now . . . . with

15. red . . . . dress

16. high . . . . . weight

17. rest . . . . fall

18. birth . . . dream

19. fare . . . . known

20. ring . . . . . . ship

  8–10 AVERAGE
11–13 GOOD
14–16 VERY GOOD
17–20 EXCEPTIONAL

Each correct answer scores one point

Part IX is a series of ten culture-free tests designed to test your powers of logical reasoning, and understanding of relationships, pattern and design. Study each display of diagrams and select the missing item from the choices given. Study the instructions given to each question.

You have ten minutes to complete the twenty questions.

Diagrammatic Representation

Example: Ɛ   is to   / / / /

as   () is to   ++ , / / / , ∞ , =

Answer: =   has the same relationship to   ()

as   / / / /   has to   Ɛ.

1. Which figure does not belong in this set?

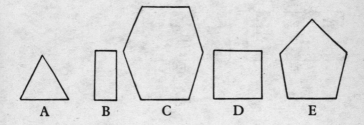

A   B   C   D   E

2.

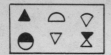   is to

as

is to:

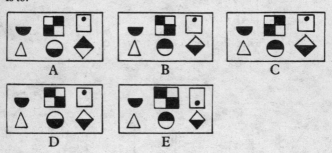

3.

Which of the five boxes below
is most like the box on the left?

A   B   C   D   E

4.

Which of the five boxes below
is most like the box on the left?

A   B   C   D   E

5. Look along each line horizontally and down each line vertically and decide from the choice given which you think should logically be the missing tile.

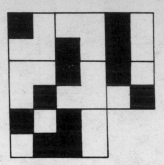

Choose from:

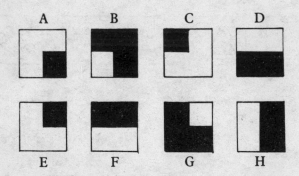

A   B   C   D

E   F   G   H

6. Look along each line horizontally and down each line vertically and decide from the choice given which you think should logically be the missing tile.

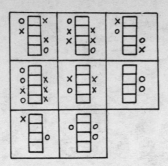

Choose from:

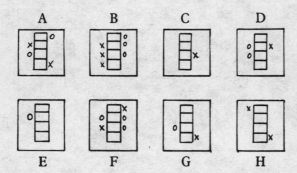

A   B   C   D

E   F   G   H

7.

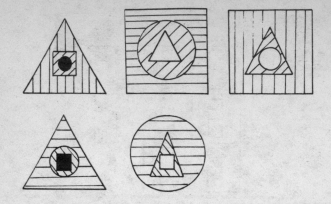

Which figure below will complete the above set?

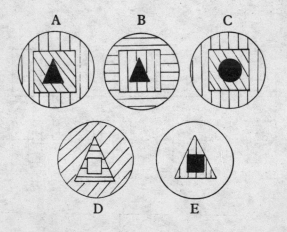

8.

  is to

as

is to:

A   B   C   D   E

9.

Which of the boxes below continues the above sequence?

A   B   C   D   E

10.

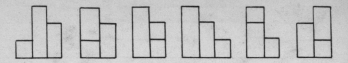

Which figure below continues the above sequence?

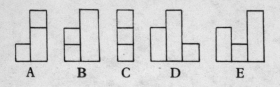

A   B   C   D   E

 8–10   **AVERAGE**
12–14   **GOOD**
16   **VERY GOOD**
18–20   **EXCEPTIONAL**

Each correct answer scores two points

Part X is a series of ten tests designed to test your powers of calculation and logic. From the alternatives given in each question choose the answer which you think is correct.

You have twenty minutes to solve the ten questions.

Example: My watch shows the time at 12.25; one clock shows 12.10. The radio announces 12.30, the church clock strikes 12.00, and your watch shows 12.15. The correct time is 12.20. What is the average time, fast or slow, as shown by these time-pieces?

A.	2 min slow	B.	4 min slow	C.	6 min slow
D.	2 min fast	E.	4 min fast	F.	6 min fast

Answer: B. 4 min slow.

1. By 8 p.m. all the party guests had arrived. By 9 p.m. a third of them had departed. By 10 p.m. a third of those remaining had also departed. By 11 p.m. the same happened again and a third of those remaining had also departed. After this only eight guests still remained at the party. How many guests were originally at the party at 8 p.m?

A.	36	B.	33	C.	30
D.	27	E.	24	F.	18

2. The cost of hiring a bus is shared equally by all the passengers. The bus has seats for 40 passengers and the total bill amounts to £70.37. How many passenger seats were not occupied?

A.	13	B.	11	C.	9
D.	7	E.	5	F.	3

3. Four different coloured counters are placed in a row. The red counter is next to the green counter but not next to the blue. The blue counter is not next to the yellow. Which counter is next to the yellow?

    A. red   B. green   C. there is insufficient evidence to determine

4. Three men, Mr Peters, Mr Edwards and Mr Roberts, were playing a round of golf together. Half-way through the game Mr Peters remarked that he had just realised that their three christian names were Peter, Edward and Robert. 'Yes', said one of the others 'I'd noticed that too, but none of us has the same surname as our own christian name—for example, my first name is Robert'. What are the full names of the three men?

   A. Edward Roberts, Peter Edwards, Robert Peters
   B. Peter Roberts, Edward Peters, Robert Edwards
   C. There is insufficient information to determine

5. How much money have you?' asked Tom's father. 'Well', replied Tom, 'if Dick gives me £4 he'll have half as much as Harry, but if Harry gives me £4 then the three of us will all have the same amount'. What was the total amount of money that Tom, Dick and Harry had between them?

   A. £27   B. £30   C. £32
   D. £36   E. £42   F. £48

6. A car travels at a speed of 20 m.p.h. over a certain distance and then returns over the same distance at a speed of 30 m.p.h. What is the average speed for the total journey?

   A. 22 m.p.h.   B. 22.5 m.p.h.   C. 23 m.p.h.
   D. 24 m.p.h.   E. 24.5 m.p.h.   F. 25 m.p.h.

7. Tom, Dick and Harry each win on the horses for three days running. The following are the nine amounts which the bookie paid out (starting with the smallest amount through to the largest amount).

   £5 — £6 — £8 — £12 — £17 — £18 — £22 — £30 — £36

   Tom won twice as much as Dick. What was the total winnings for Harry over the three days?

   A. £25   B. £35   C. £45
   D. £55   E. £65   F. £75

8. A train travelling at a speed of 45 m.p.h. enters a tunnel which is 1.5 miles long. The length of the train is 0.75 mile. How long does it take for all of the train to pass through the tunnel from the moment the front of the train enters the tunnel to the moment the rear emerges?

A. 1.8 min   B. 2 min   C 2.5 min
D. 3 min   E. 3.18 min   F. 3.25 min

9. If a car had increased its average speed for a 210-mile journey by 5 m.p.h. the journey would have been completed in one hour less. What was the original speed of the car for the journey?

A. 28 m.p.h.   B. 30 m.p.h.   C. 31 m.p.h.
D. 32 m.p.h.   E. 33 m.p.h.   F. 36 m.p.h.

10. Below are three statements by snooker players. At least one of the statements is false and at least one is true.

i)   DAVIS: 'Taylor did not pot the black'
ii) TAYLOR: 'I did not pot the black'
iii) HIGGINS: 'I potted the black'

Who did pot the black?
A. Davis   B. Taylor   C. Higgins

8–10   AVERAGE
12–14 GOOD
16   VERY GOOD
18–20 EXCEPTIONAL

Each correct answer scores two points

TEST TWO • ANSWERS

TEST TWO • PART I
1. cavity 2. marine 3. strike 4. ink 5. cell 6. fail
7. arrival 8. size 9. dale 10. arsonist 11. index
12. dress 13. rash 14. argue 15. challenge 16. verdant
17. medium 18. virile 19. parole 20. sever

TEST TWO • PART II
1. comfortable 2. rash 3. factual 4. resolute
5. common 6. comfort 7. dulcet 8. sickness 9. chief
10. sedate 11. base 12. reluctant 13. obvious
14. tycoon 15. description 16. specification 17. story
18. offer 19. viable 20. braid

TEST TWO • PART III
1. depression 2. gentle 3. illicit 4. enhance 5. giddy
6. cloak 7. receive 8. common 9. chaos 10. loosen
11. spurious 12. salubrious 13. pollute 14. wickedness
15. commend 16. stout 17. querulous 18. apathy
19. prudent 20. dim

TEST TWO • PART IV
1. cloth 2. legs 3. emotion 4. churlish 5. vase
6. weight 7. please 8. rodent 9. hush 10. withdraw
11. father 12. false 13. decrease 14. disaster 15. cyan
16. animals 17. cattle 18. land 19. meeting
20. armada

TEST TWO • PART V
1. dispute, doubt 2. mild, serene 3. mount,
peak 4. scare, alarm 5. lively, bouncy 6. sensual,
erotic 7. remote, far 8. drizzle, deluge 9. tense,
strained 10. crush, grind 11. elation, glee 12. assign,
designate 13. sign, indication 14. retreat,
haven 15. apparition, phantom 16. doodle,

scrawl   17. costume, regalia   18. myriad,
multitude   19. staid, sober   20. adore, cherish

TEST TWO • PART VI
1. wise, absurd   2. resign, stay   3. portly, puny   4. alter,
maintain   5. disperse, assemble   6. honest,
false   7. dejected, happy   8. mislay, find   9. mourn,
rejoice   10. noble, humble   11. compassion,
ruthlessness   12. fracture, union   13. vivid,
dull   14. patient, restive   15. penitent,
unrepentant   16. facetious, serious   17. conclude,
introduce   18. append, remove   19. defamation,
praise   20. resent, condone

TEST TWO • PART VII
1. snarl   2. lag   3. stick   4. rare   5. scale   6. punch
7. last   8. shock   9. bail   10. boom   11. crane   12. key
13. perch   14. temple   15. admit   16. case   17. firm
18. riddle   19. rifle   20. vamp

TEST TWO • PART VIII
1. way   2. guard   3. skin   4. stream   5. made
6. range   7. lace   8. stick   9. land   10. stone
11. card   12. back   13. table   14. here   15. head
16. light   17. rain   18. day   19. well   20. leader

TEST TWO • PART IX
1. B	6. C
2. B	7. A
3. C	8. C
4. A	9. B
5. G	10. E

TEST TWO • PART X

1. D. 27
2. C. 9
3. A. red
4. B. Peter Roberts, Edward Peters,
   Robert Edwards
5. D. £36

6. D. 24 m.p.h.
7. D. £55
8. D. 3 min
9. B. 30 m.p.h.
10. A. Davis

TOTAL SCORE

80–100	AVERAGE
101–130	GOOD
131–160	VERY GOOD
161–200	EXCEPTIONAL

TEST THREE

Part I is a series of twenty questions designed to test your ability in collecting together objects or ideas which belong to a set, or have some common attribute. To make this classification simpler we have put together a series of words and you have to spot the 'odd one out'. There are five words and only four of them have a common theme; underline the '<u>odd one</u>'.

You have ten minutes to complete the twenty questions.

Classification

Example: bag, basket, <u>hat</u>, pocket, bucket

Answer: <u>hat</u>, the other four are used for carrying things.

1. potato, turnip, beetroot, carrot, pea
2. cygnet, kitten, chick, puppy, cockerel
3. corner, chimney, nook, cranny, niche
4. cut, carve, cramp, chisel, chip
5. corporal, captain, sergeant, commodore, private
6. renter, squatter, hirer, lessee, tenant
7. cornea, uvula, retina, eyelid, eyelash
8. ocarina, cello, harp, double-bass, viola
9. Bradford, York, Grimsby, Harrogate, Filey
10. gale, hurricane, tycoon, wind, breeze
11. beret, panama, stetson, trilby, Pandora
12. sanguine, viridescent, vermilion, crimson, scarlet
13. turkey, chicken, Bombay duck, capon, goose
14. Keats, Elgar, Masefield, Shelley, Wordsworth
15. black, brown, grey, green, pink
16. Vermont, Alberta, Utah, Colorado, Oklahoma
17. alpha, gamma, thuja, iota, epsilon
18. Degas, Helpmann, Nureyev, Nijinsky, Sleep
19. Bering, South China, Yellow, Caribbean, Congo
20. circle, reredos, fauteuil, balcony, stalls

8–10	AVERAGE
11–13	GOOD
14–16	VERY GOOD
17–20	EXCEPTIONAL

Each correct answer scores one point

Part II is a series of twenty questions designed to test your knowledge of language and your ability to spot words which have the same meaning. We have grouped together five words and from them you have to underline the <u>word</u> which means the same or has the closest meaning to the KEY word.

You have ten minutes to complete the twenty questions.

Example: ANGULAR (blunt, stiff, abrupt, <u>branching</u>, cornered)

Answer: <u>branching</u> is the word closest in meaning to the <u>KEY</u> word, ANGULAR.

1. MAXIM (saying, prize, comic, brittle, scheme)
2. CORPULENT (piece, gross, soldier, shade, sea-bird)
3. SCOURGE (scrub, miser, dried, bane, plead)
4. GAUNT (lean, falcon, greyish, glove, follow)
5. RUFFIAN (villain, untidy, trifle, idiot, picture)
6. RESOLUTE (promise, steady, gamble, solid, solution)
7. WHEEDLE (prune, travel, evacuate, stoke, coax)
8. SUPPRESS (weight, hedge, stifle, smooth, yearn)
9. ADMONISH (spill, disappear, caution, gleam, certain)
10. BESEECH (carve, encircle, kneel, pray, written)
11. ACQUIESCE (wonder, disbelieve, agree, follow, direct)
12. COMMISERATE (converse, pardon, pity, ignore, mix)
13. LIGATURE (proceedings, legal aid, puncture, bandage, picture)
14. MELIORATE (improve, sweeten, hasten, obstruct, promise)
15. ORLOP (deck, jewel, bird, fish, rock)
16. JARGON (foreign, wagon, tub, lingo, jolt)
17. HEINOUS (nervous, plea, odious, spontaneous, lofty)
18. TURBID (engine, thick, auction, annoint, quarrel)
19. NECROMANCY (healing, romancing, witchcraft, hating, wishing)
20. CHIMERA (cloak, monster, bauble, ornament, clock)

8–10 AVERAGE
11–13 GOOD
14–16 VERY GOOD
17–20 EXCEPTIONAL

Each correct answer scores one point

Part III is a series of twenty questions designed to test your knowledge of language and your ability to visualise opposite meanings quickly. We have grouped together five words and from them you have to underline the <u>word</u> which means the opposite or is as nearly as possible opposite in meaning to the KEY word.

You have ten minutes to complete the twenty questions.

Antonyms

Example: CARELESS (exact, <u>heedful</u>, strict, anxious, dutiful)

Answer: <u>heedful</u> is the word which means the opposite of
the KEY word CARELESS.

1. CRONY (friend, enemy, partner, stranger, brother)
2. FEARLESS (afraid, qualm, shuffle, comfort, doubtful)
3. SPARKLING (witty, shame, victory, dull, awful)
4. LOVING (seraphic, fiendish, hateful, childish, frightful)
5. BOGUS (spiteful, game, manage, true, chasm)
6. ENLIGHTEN (wrap, emit, mystify, unload, strike)
7. IMPARTIAL (concealed, dressed, biased, displayed, loaded)
8. UNFETTER (gambol, wager, tire, tether, castigate)
9. IMPEACH (stoned, flounder, calm, insulate, acquit)
10. SCARCITY (beggarly, pretence, liberate, plenty, disappearance)
11. BARREN (effete, theatre, frayed, enclose, fertile)
12. PENALISE (senile, image, remunerate, check, defraud)

13. REPROACH (approve, set, gangway, frighten, enquire)
14. KINDLE (enfold, respect, father, advance, extinguish)
15. ABSOLVE (convict, soften, fixture, reply, lessen)
16. COLLABORATE (collect, sell, hinder, withdraw, connect)
17. MALEVOLENT (friendly, ugly, difficult, splendid, shady)
18. CARNIVOROUS (cavernous, vegetarian, proletarian, misanthropic, calm)
19. PAUCITY (slenderness, rigid, game, pinched, abundance)
20. TURBULENCE (generating, placidness, changing, uproar, hubbub)

8–10   AVERAGE
11–13   GOOD
14–16   VERY GOOD
17–20   EXCEPTIONAL

Each correct answer scores one point

Part IV is a series of twenty questions designed to test your ability to visualise relationships between various objects and ideas. We have grouped together five words, one of which will pair up with the KEY word to produce a similar relationship to the two-word example. Underline the <u>word</u> which is appropriate.

You have ten minutes to complete the twenty questions.

Analogy

Example: TIRED is to work as
HAPPY is to (sleep, rest, <u>success</u>, exercise, eating)

Answer: <u>success</u> has a similar relationship to HAPPY as work has to TIRED.

1. GUILLOTINE is to neck as
   SHEARS are to (sharpen, hedge, cut, implement, steel)

2. MEDIUM is to seance as
   ACTOR is to (make-up, costume, performance, artist, music)

3. SKATER is to ice as
   DANCER is to (foxtrot, band, ballroom, dress, steps)

4. CIRCLE is to sphere as
   SQUARE is to (triangle, cube, hexagonal, oblong, hemisphere)

5. A is to J as
   TWO is to (seven, nine, eleven, thirteen, fifteen)

6. NEEDLE is to thread as
   PEN is to (write, hand, express, ink, letter)

7. NURSE is to hospital as
   PEDAGOGUE is to (factory, learning, school, examination, study)

8. ROSE is to England as
   THISTLE is to (Wales, sting, Scotland, meadow, Ireland)

9. ROAD is to tarmacadam as
   SOIL is to (trees, weeds, grass, stones, rubble)

10. BEAUFORT is to wind as
    VERNIER is to (weather, poet, scale, wine, politician)

11. FARRIER is to horseshoes as
    CARTOGRAPHER is to (leather, glass, maps, pottery, gold)

12. LOZENGE is to capsule as
    PUCK is to (circle, sphere, square, oval, triangle)

13. OPTICIAN is to eyes as
    GERIATRIC is to (young, old, foreign, insular, needy)

14. HANDS are to clockwise as
    PENDULUM is to (vertical, time, clock, alternating, swings)

15. BEDLAM is to lunatic as
    HOLLOWAY is to (madman, child, woman, jail, magistrate)

16. CHAUFFEUR is to limousine as
    MAHOUT is to (elephant, camel, horse, rickshaw, sedan-chair)

17. RUBBISH is to tip as
    JETSAM is to (sea, beach, dustbin, roadway, pasture)

18. CUNEIFORM is to wedge as
    ALIFORM is to (club, spade, diamond, heart, wing)

19. LAPWING is to desert as
    OWLS are to (parliament, birds, hoot, trees, fly)

20. FUNAMBULIST is to tightrope-walker as
    SOMNAMBULIST is to (hiker, sportsman, sleep-walker, archer, golfer)

8–10   AVERAGE
11–13 GOOD
14–16 VERY GOOD
17–20 EXCEPTIONAL

Each correct answer scores one point

TEST THREE • PART V

Part V is a series of twenty questions designed to test your knowledge of language and your ability to quickly recognise words of similar meanings. There are six words in each question and you have to find a pair of words which have similar meanings. Underline the two words which you believe to be closest in meaning.

You have ten minutes to complete the twenty questions.

Example: <u>walk</u>, run drive, <u>stroll</u>, fly, sit

Answer: <u>walk</u> and <u>stroll</u> are the two words in the list
          which are closest in meaning.

1. thick, beginner, misery, turpid, banish, lucky
2. stewed, punished, zeal, deserted, felt, ardour
3. cascade, relish, fruitful, zest, mute, scene
4. beastly, uniform, magical, famine, livery, lowly
5. compunction, common, meeting, regret, grammar, feeling
6. default, baffle, foil, silvery, sound, resist
7. thicket, unwise, body, welcome, collect, copse
8. reply, delight, kindle, related, ignite, proposal
9. cover, ward, watch, alien, house, manage
10. farce, gambol, sheepish, frolic, wager, fixture
11. justice, real, perfect, follow, equity, insurance
12. tread, measure, mete, discover, wealth, trend
13. perforate, written, caste, liberate, align, bored
14. convoy, vehicle, hold, meander, relate, escort
15. pitiful, wonder, chill, awful, terrible, used
16. dabble, concept, mix, idiot, trifle, perfect
17. unmoving, defile, sculptor, statute, law, marble
18. fussy, yearn, long, memorise, woven, pelt
19. trickle, creek, ardent, exceptional, drip, difficult
20. brake, earthy, quaver, vibrate, settle, shake

8–10	AVERAGE
11–13	GOOD
14–16	VERY GOOD
17–20	EXCEPTIONAL

Each correct answer scores one point

Part VI is a series of twenty questions designed to test your knowledge of language and your ability to quickly recognise words of opposite meaning. There are six words in each question and you have to find a pair of words which have opposite meanings. Underline the <u>two words</u> which you believe to be opposite in meaning.

You have ten minutes to complete the twenty questions.

Example: curved, long, <u>big</u>, <u>small</u>, broad, fat

Answer: <u>big</u> and <u>small</u> are the two words in the list which are opposite in meaning.

1. uniform, pleasure, praise, deed, irregular, mistake
2. grotesque, horror, giant, nuptual, attraction, meaningful
3. crazy, attack, measure, mix, assort, generous
4. colourful, slender, grim, awesome, sprightly, beautiful
5. desperate, gathered, straight, forlorn, cherished, crumpled
6. pagan, exotic, moving, civilised, hungry, calmed
7. chop, outstrip, teach, use, follow, uncover
8. starlight, ancient, period, blacken, infinity, definition
9. axed, blocked, listened, fathom, wondered, cubed
10. exhale, cheat, adore, follow, harness, elude
11. alley, render, occult, blacken, brew, open
12. help, delight, pain, sweetmeat, halo, grandeur
13. feature, failure, sharp, system, picture, stature
14. cynical, leaning, cone, lenient, comical, uncouth
15. emergency, hurtful, underhand, provision, storey, ambush
16. triangle, thoroughfare, ogre, perfection, treasure, deformity
17. tickle, fate, enlighten, fiery, tame, fear
18. tissue, unsoiled, dirty, transparent, trace, simple
19. knitted, naked, staring, draped, slither, dumped
20. print, reap, patronise, audience, oppress, bind

8–10	AVERAGE	14–16	VERY GOOD
11–13	GOOD	17–20	EXCEPTIONAL

Each correct answer scores one point

Part VII is a series of twenty questions designed to test your ability to quickly find alternative meanings of words. You are looking for a word which has the same meaning as one word or phrase in one sense, and the same meaning as a different word or phrase in another sense. The dots represent the number of letters in the missing word. Fill in the missing word.

You have twenty minutes to complete the twenty questions.

Double Meanings

Example: breathes heavily . . . . . underclothes

Answer: pants.

1. engrave . . . . . pursue

2. slow the motion . . . . . crossed-line pattern

3. disregard . . . . deduction from amount

4. struggle and plunge . . . . flat-fish

5. candid . . . . . mark letter

6. precipitate flight . . . . coal-box

7. perpendicular . . . . . deviate from course

86

8. wax candle . . . . .   grow gradually less

9. line of people . . . . .   plaited hair

10. swimming bird . . . .   untwilled linen

11. sleeping berth . . . .   vanish

12. break apart . . . . .   adhere to

13. bird of prey . . . .   plasterer's board

14. make angry . . . . . .   sweet-smelling gum

15. to reserve in advance . . . .   literary composition

16. young animals at birth . . . . .   waste paper
    strewn about

17. long pole used to support TV camera . . . .   speak
    with deep resonant sound

18. cylindrical hand warmer . . . .   stupid person

19. to run away . . . .   short, heavy arrow

20. powdered tobacco . . . . .   charred part of
    candlewick

 8–10 AVERAGE
11–13 GOOD
14–16 VERY GOOD
17–20 EXCEPTIONAL

Each correct answer scores one point

Part VIII is a series of twenty questions designed to test your ability at innovation. You are given the first part of the word or phrase, and you have to find the second part. The same second part then becomes the first part of a second word or phrase. The dots represent the number of letters in the missing word. Fill in the missing word.

You have twenty minutes to complete the twenty questions.

Double Words

Example: house . . . . all

Answer: hold.

1. cricket . . . . . stick

2. tee . . . . . tail

3. merry . . . . stocking

4. looking . . . . . eye

5. sheet . . . . . hall

6. general . . . . bed

7. seaside . . . . cake

8. book . . . . time

9. fly . . . . tackle

10. hold . . . . . fit

11. ice . . . . . bun

12. candle . . . . . insect

13. table . . . . light

14. flick . . . . . sharpener

15. cows . . . . churn

16. open . . . . . wife

17. happy . . . . party

18. crows . . . . stool

19. house . . . . . wall

20. lobster . . . hole

8–10   AVERAGE
11–13   GOOD
14–16   VERY GOOD
17–20   EXCEPTIONAL

Each correct answer scores one point

TEST THREE • PART IX

Part IX is a series of ten culture-free tests designed to test your powers of logical reasoning, and understanding of relationships, pattern and design. Study each display of diagrams and select the missing item from the choices given. Study the instructions given to each question.

You have twenty minutes to complete the ten questions.

Diagrammatic Representation

Example: Ɛ   is to   / I I I

as   ()   is to   ++ , III , OO , =

Answer: =   has the same relationship to   ()

as   / I I I   has to   Ɛ .

1.

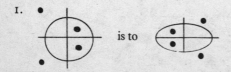

is to

as

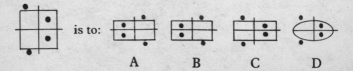

is to: A   B   C   D

2.

C	F
J	O

is to

F	J
O	C

as

D	H
M	S

is to:

H	M
S	H

A

M	H
Z	B

B

H	M
S	D

C

M	H
Y	D

D

3.

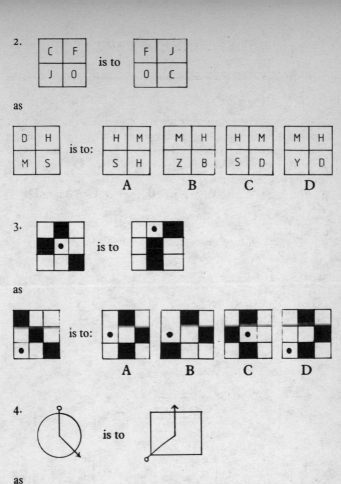

4.

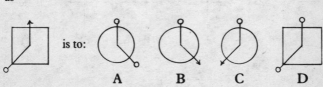

91

5.

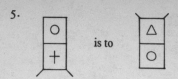 is to

as

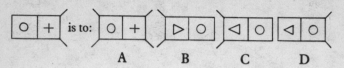

              A   B   C   D

6.

is to

as

is to:

              A   B   C   D

7.

4	3
8	7

is to

28	24
5	3

as

2	3
6	7

is to:

18	14
5	3

A

14	18
5	3

B

14	18
3	5

C

18	14
3	5

D

8.

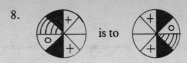

as

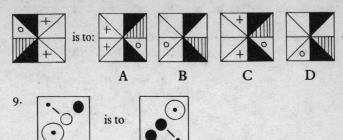

A   B   C   D

9.

as

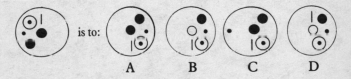

A   B   C   D

10.

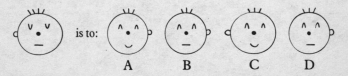

as

A   B   C   D

| 8–10 | AVERAGE | 16 | VERY GOOD |
| 12–14 | GOOD | 18–20 | EXCEPTIONAL |

Each correct answer scores two points

93

Part X is a series of ten tests designed to test your powers of calculation and logic. From the alternatives given in each question choose the answer which you think is correct.

You have twenty minutes in which to solve the ten questions.

Example: My watch shows the time at 12.25; one clock shows 12.10. The radio announces 12.30, the church clock strikes 12.00, and your watch shows 12.15. The correct time is 12.20. What is the average time, fast or slow, as shown by these time-pieces?

A. 2 min slow   B. 4 min slow   C. 6 min slow
D. 2 min fast   E. 4 min fast   F. 6 min fast

Answer: **B.** 4 min slow.

1. What is the difference between 9 metres square and 9 square metres?

   A. 0 sq.m.   B. 9 sq.m.   C. 56 sq.m.
   D. 72 sq.m.   E. 144 sq.m

2. What is the missing number:

   1   8   27   X   125   216?

   A. 36   B. 64   C. 80   D. 100
   E. 112

3. What is the missing number:

   1   9   36   100   X   441?

   A. 185   B. 195   C. 205
   D. 215   E. 225

4. What is the answer to the following calculation: 9 × 99 × 999?

   A. 809109   B. 890019   C. 980019
   D. 98109   E. 890109

5. The houses in a street are numbered 1, 2, 3, 4 etc. up one side, then back down the other side. Opposite No. 10 is No. 23. How many houses in the street?

A. 31   B. 32   C. 33   D. 34
E. 35

6. What fraction has to be added to ⅜ to make it equal ⅔?

A. 5/24   B. 7/24   C. 9/24
D. 9/16   E. 11/30

7. If three apples and four oranges cost 40p and four apples and three oranges cost 37p, how much does one orange cost?

A. 4p   B. 5p   C. 6p   D. 7p
E. 8p

8. What is the square root of 729?

A. 27   B. 33   C. 37   D. 43
E. 47

9. Nineteen players enter a tennis tournament on a knock-out basis; some players will have a bye for the first round to bring the number down to sixteen for the second round. How many matches will be played?

A. 17   B. 18   C. 19   D. 20
E. 21

10. What is the next number in this sequence?

    11   13   17   25   32

A. 36   B. 37   C. 38   D. 39
E. 40

8–10	AVERAGE	16	VERY GOOD
12–14	GOOD	18–20	EXCEPTIONAL

Each correct answer scores two points

TEST THREE • PART I
1. pea   2. cockerel   3. chimney   4. cramp
5. commodore   6. squatter   7. uvula   8. ocarina
9. Grimsby   10. tycoon   11. Pandora   12. viridescent
13. Bombay duck   14. Elgar   15. grey   16. Alberta
17. thuja   18. Degas   19. Congo   20. reredos

TEST THREE • PART II
1. saying   2. gross   3. scrub   4. lean   5. villain
6. steady   7. coax   8. stifle   9. caution   10. pray
11. agree   12. pity   13. bandage   14. improve   15. deck
16. lingo   17. odious   18. thick   19. witchcraft
20. monster

TEST THREE • PART III
1. enemy   2. afraid   3. dull   4. hateful   5. true
6. mystify   7. biased   8. tether   9. acquit   10. plenty
11. fertile   12. remunerate   13. approve   14. extinguish
15. convict   16. hinder   17. friendly   18. vegetarian
19. abundance   20. placidness

TEST THREE • PART IV
1. hedge   2. performance   3. ballroom   4. cube
5. eleven   6. ink   7. school   8. Scotland   9. grass
10. scale   11. maps   12. sphere   13. old   14. alternating
15. woman   16. elephant   17. beach   18. wing
19. parliament   20. sleep-walker

TEST THREE • PART V
1. thick, turpid   2. zeal, ardour   3. relish,
zest   4. uniform, livery   5. compunction, regret   6. baffle,
foil   7. thicket, copse   8. kindle, ignite   9. ward,
watch   10. gambol, frolic   11. justice, equity   12. measure,
mete   13. perforate, bored   14. convoy, escort   15. awful,

terrible 16. dabble, trifle 17. statute, law 18. yearn,
long 19. trickle, drip 20. vibrate, shake

TEST THREE ● PART VI
1. uniform, irregular 2. horror, attraction 3. mix,
assort 4. grim, beautiful 5. forlorn, cherished 6. pagan,
civilised 7. outstrip, follow 8. period,
infinity 9. blocked, fathom 10. follow, elude 11. occult,
open 12. delight, pain 13. feature, system 14. cynical,
lenient 15. emergency, provision 16. perfection,
deformity 17. fiery, tame 18. unsoiled, dirty 19. naked,
draped 20. patronise, oppress

TEST THREE ● PART VII
1. chase 2. check 3. discount 4. flounder 5. frank
6. scuttle 7. sheer 8. taper 9. queue 10. duck
11. bunk 12. cleave 13. hawk 14. incense 15. book
16. litter 17. boom 18. muff 19. bolt 20. snuff

TEST THREE ● PART VIII
1. match 2. shirt 3. Christmas 4. glass 5. music
6. hospital 7. rock 8. mark 9. fishing 10. tight
11. cream 12. stick 13. lamp 14. knife 15. milk
16. house 17. birthday 18. foot 19. brick 20. pot

TEST THREE ● PART IX
1. B   6. B
2. C   7. C
3. A   8. C
4. B   9. B
5. C   10. A

TEST THREE ● PART X
1. D. 72 sq.m.   6. B. 7/24
2. B. 64   7. D. 7p
3. E. 225   8. A. 27
4. E. 890109   9. B. 18
5. B. 32   10. B. 37

TOTAL SCORE

80–100   AVERAGE
101–130 GOOD
131–160 VERY GOOD
161–200 EXCEPTIONAL

TEST FOUR

Part I is a series of twenty questions designed to test your ability in collecting together objects or ideas which belong to a set, or have some common attribute. To make this classification simpler we have put together a series of words and you have to spot the 'odd one out'. There are five words and only four of them have a common theme; underline the '<u>odd one</u>'.

You have ten minutes to complete the twenty questions.

Classification

Example: bag, basket, <u>hat</u>, pocket, bucket

Answer: <u>hat</u>, the other four are used for carrying things.

1. walk, stroll, run, amble, dawdle
2. football, netball, hockey, rugby, cricket
3. lake, pond, sea, mere, pool
4. boy, man, king, lad, queen
5. ballpen, crayon, chalk, pencil, paintbrush
6. minim, crotchet, breve, denim, quaver
7. square, triangle, hexagon, rectangle, cube
8. rain, sleet, hail, snow, wind
9. sage, onion, thyme, sorrel, basil
10. lion, wolf, kangaroo, tiger, zebra
11. wool, cotton, nylon, silk, denim
12. aster, wallflower, tulip, petunia, hollyhock
13. chair, stool, sofa, settee, pew
14. tiredness, recuperation, lassitude, languor, weariness
15. tin, bronze, zinc, gold, silver
16. sextant, verger, chaplain, presbyter, minister
17. rack, thumbscrew, pilliwinks, wheel, guillotine
18. snickersnee, misericord, carronade, poniard, scimitar
19. mahogany, pine, oak, rosewood, beech
20. parabola, catenary, hyperbola, circle, oval

8–10   AVERAGE
11–13 GOOD
14–16 VERY GOOD
17–20 EXCEPTIONAL

Each correct answer scores one point

Part II is a series of twenty questions designed to test your knowledge of language and your ability to spot words which have the same meaning. We have grouped together five words and from them you have to underline the <u>word</u> which means the same or has the closest meaning to the KEY word.

You have ten minutes to complete the twenty questions.

Synonyms

Example: ANGULAR (blunt, stiff, abrupt, <u>branching</u>, cornered)

Answer: <u>branching</u> is the word closest in meaning to the KEY word, ANGULAR.

1. CONSTRICT (build, interpret, endure, compress, embarrass)
2. MANIKIN (sketch, poser, dwarf, mannish, spirit)
3. SANGUINE (restful, stale, cool, confident, cooked)
4. TENUITY (continual, lasting, slenderness, sinuous, boldness)
5. CONCORDANT (aviator, mixture, coincident, complex, harmonious)
6. SMIRCH (smile, expression, smear, liqueur, stumble)
7. ONEROUS (heavy, burdensome, honourable, leafless, dreamlike)
8. INVEIGLE (abuse, plot, tempt, smother, cheat)

9. DELECTABLE (edible, pleasant, inviting, helpful, juicy)
10. ANNUNCIATOR (anointer, punisher, demonstrator, announcer, destructor)
11. GOBBET (piece, melon, elf, mouth, fastener)
12. IMPALPABLE (battered, intangible, pinned, stubborn, fruitless)
13. ARCHAIC (bow-like, superior, chaotic, primitive, lasting)
14. ASSIDUOUS (begging, persevering, acidity, declare, reasonable)
15. OSCITATION (yawning, twisting, rubbing, winking, oscillating)
16. TIMBAL (cask, quality, kettledrum, forest, reserved)
17. PASTICHE (medley, cake, painting, lozenge, group)
18. APPRISE (promote, lift, reward, inform, write)
19. COLLOCATE (cancel, brew, master, arrange, locate)
20. CONTROVERT (disrespect, deny, fight, exception, oppose)

8–10   AVERAGE
11–13 GOOD
14–16 VERY GOOD
17–20 EXCEPTIONAL

Each correct answer scores one point

Part III is a series of twenty questions designed to test your knowledge of language and your ability to visualise opposite meanings quickly. We have grouped together five words and from them you have to underline the <u>word</u> which means the opposite or is as nearly as possible opposite in meaning to the KEY word.

You have ten minutes to complete the twenty questions.

Antonyms

Example: CARELESS (exact, <u>heedful</u>, strict, anxious, dutiful)
Answer: <u>heedful</u> is the word which means the opposite of the KEY word CARELESS.

1. SCREEN (dispel, shield, expose, enquire, sneer)
2. UNIFORM (invest, redress, diverse, level, straight)
3. READY (slow, loth, dutiful, crawl, begin)
4. LIBERAL (labour, mean, plentiful, great, showy)
5. CONFUSION (disarray, upright, rigid, order, opportunity)
6. DWINDLE (fade, increase, support, return, obscure)
7. CAPTURE (imprison, suppose, import, desire, elude)
8. INSUBORDINATE (mutinous, thoughtless, obedient, humorous, bright)
9. SPURN (juggle, wish, welcome, conduct, show)
10. VOLATILE (standing, sluggish, pivoting, shielding, vacant)
11. COGNISANT (seeing, smartness, brittle, fond, ignorant)
12. GLOAMING (dawn, valley, river, hill, rain)
13. AFFLUENCE (charming, poverty, ugly, influence, flowing)
14. PROFANE (ugly, sacred, indifferent, backward, portly)
15. CAVERNOUS (rocky, smooth, shaky, porous, cramped)
16. LIMPID (straight, loose, obscure, shady, benevolent)
17. NOXIOUS (notorious, benign, anxious, irritating, slow)
18. HISPID (uneven, bright, smooth, wrinkled, steep)
19. COGENT (believable, unconvincing, sure, exact, indifferent)
20. INDIGENOUS (foreign, digestible, deep, deceptive, belonging)

| 8–10 | AVERAGE | 14–16 | VERY GOOD |
| 11–13 | GOOD | 17–20 | EXCEPTIONAL |

Each correct answer scores one point

TEST FOUR • PART IV

Part IV is a series of twenty questions designed to test your
ability to visualise relationships between various objects and
ideas. We have grouped together five words, one of which will
pair up with the KEY word to produce a similar relationship to
the two-word example. Underline the <u>word</u> which is appropriate.

You have ten minutes to complete the twenty questions.

Analogy

Example: **TIRED** is to work as
        HAPPY is to (sleep, rest, <u>success</u>, exercise, eating)
Answer: <u>success</u> has a similar relationship to HAPPY as work
        has to TIRED.

1. **CARPET** is to floor as
   CURTAIN is to (hang, glass, window, hide, cover)

2. **ROAD** is to car as
   SEA is to (island, fish, iceberg, ship, seaweed)

3. **HOT** is to cold as
   FLORID is to (pallid, garden, treasure, bouquet, face)

4. **HARPOON** is to whale as
   LANCE is to (horse, soldier, bull, knight, fight)

5. **BOOK** is to library as
   PAINTING is to (artist, gallery, colour, brush, critic)

6. SAN FRANCISCO is to California as
   PORTLAND is to (Georgia, Indiana, Oregon, Arizona, Utah)

7. GAG is to mouth as
   BLINDFOLD is to (cover, pad, eyes, mask, blank)

8. QUIET is to calm as
   ORDER is to (peace, force, sort, march, line)

9. SINGERS are to choir as
   DANCERS are to (theatre, troupe, class, style, clap)

10. HARD is to rock as
    SOFT is to (slate, paper, glass, sponge, lead)

11. ANOINT is to baptise as
    INJECT is to (treat, settle, innoculate, pinch, heal)

12. DUKEDOM is to nobility as
    MOTHER is to (brother, family, class, type, sister)

13. BISHOP is to chess-board as
    SOLDIER is to (army, colonel, battlefield, uniform, rifle)

14. LESSEE is to house as
    HEIRESS is to (bankrupt, Earl, fortune, nobility, senile)

15. SANDPAPER is to smoothness as
    HALF-NELSON is to (tackle, hornpipe, sailing, laying, stranglehold)

16. HOSPITAL is to curing as
    PILLORY is to (profit, praising, punishment, lending, soothing)

17. RAT is to rodent as
    KANGAROO is to (tail, marsupial, jump, sycophant, Australia)

18. **SOLICITOR** is to adviser as
    SYCOPHANT is to (ruffian, fawner, nobleman, blackmailer, flautist)

19. **GRASS** is to verdant as
    BANANA is to (heliotrope, puce, celeste, azure, yellowish)

20. **OSTRACISM** is to boycott as
    CLANDESTINE is to (secret, cheap, silent, huge, chance)

8–10 AVERAGE
11–13 GOOD
14–16 VERY GOOD
17–20 EXCEPTIONAL

Each correct answer scores one point

TEST FOUR • PART V

Part V is a series of twenty questions designed to test your knowledge of language and your ability to quickly recognise words of similar meanings. There are six words in each question and you have to find a pair of words which have similar meanings. Underline the <u>two words</u> which you believe to be closest in meaning.

You have ten minutes to complete the twenty questions.

Synonyms II

Example: <u>walk</u>, run, drive, <u>stroll</u>, fly, sit

Answer: <u>walk</u> and <u>stroll</u> are the two words in the list
which are closest in meaning.

1. ludicrous, gamesmanship, oily, absolute, absurd, obscure
2. hilarious, amazing, turbulent, corpulent, organic, tumultuous
3. idea, rotation, steamed, compulsion, propel, duress
4. freedom, ecstasy, superior, rapture, ghostly, imagination
5. tranquil, pale, sedate, aristocratic, glazed, proud
6. priceless, speedy, superb, notable, remarkable, oration
7. practice, descant, melody, bottle, trot, despair
8. recovered, traced, complicated, involuted, tangible, loaded
9. clan, tilth, wealth, cultivation, lowered, uncouth
10. petulant, straight, rusty, proud, sickening, irritable
11. swerve, arch, dike, create, dodge, edge
12. macerate, slice, discover, chew, steep, select
13. steal, broach, manage, adorn, disperse, suggest
14. harbinger, forerunner, enemy, athlete, drunkard, listener
15. fretful, listless, unhappy, register, sinking, languid
16. rummage, wander, hasten, search, scarecrow, foliage
17. loathe, writhe, squirm, wrongful, squeeze, cease
18. blacken, glossal, matched, enormous, tendon, lingual
19. becket, vase, holdall, capture, hook, jacket
20. bedspread, loiter, plank, counter, order, parry

8–10 AVERAGE
11–13 GOOD
14–16 VERY GOOD
17–20 EXCEPTIONAL

Each correct answer scores one point

Part VI is a series of twenty questions designed to test your knowledge of language and your ability to quickly recognise words of opposite meaning. There are six words in each question and you have to find a pair of words which have opposite meanings. Underline the <u>two words</u> which you believe to be opposite in meaning.

You have ten minutes to complete the twenty questions.

Example: curved, long, **big**, small, broad, flat

Answer: big and small are the two words in the list which are opposite in meaning.

1. specific, helpful, strong, knowing, innocent, confident
2. pummel, modification, joining, retention, disability, attention
3. prize, tasteful, imbue, texture, invest, clear
4. finalist, packing, artful, insolent, polite, recipe
5. excite, obtrude, wave, stem, bannister, retire
6. encourage, crime, endorse, repudiate, disappoint, halt
7. expensive, jade, sanction, glitter, enthuse, govern
8. fibre, parent, cripple, debility, frustrate, cask
9. increase, fantasy, declare, fallacy, reserve, truth
10. voted, majority, basis, esteem, craft, honesty
11. debate, sailed, prepare, export, consume, insert
12. martial, speciality, cover, peaceful, foreign, editor
13. experiment, distort, overlooked, modern, adviser, past
14. justice, edit, abdicate, occupy, court, attempt
15. defence, encourage, member, exposure, situation, freedom
16. upheld, canvass, argue, disagree, pass, shown
17. patterned, ancient, question, asleep, prosaic, poetic
18. depose, puritan, break, tart, suave, sport
19. bale, leader, stagnant, watery, flag, brisk
20. whet, ruled, arid, nauseate, elect, chance

8–10	AVERAGE	14–16	VERY GOOD
11–13	GOOD	17–20	EXCEPTIONAL

Each correct answer scores one point

Part VII is a series of twenty questions designed to test your ability to quickly find alternative meanings of words. You are looking for a word which has the same meaning as one word or phrase in one sense, and the same meaning as a different word or phrase in another sense. The dots represent the number of letters in the missing word. Fill in the missing word.

You have twenty minutes to complete the twenty questions.

Double Meanings

Example: breathes heavily . . . . underclothes

Answer: pants.

1. a flower . . . . ascended

2. part of railway track . . . . small amphibian

3. dance assembly . . . . hard or soft sphere used for games

4. broth . . . . . in store

5. excavation to receive corpse . . . . . needing serious thought

6. small wooden building . . . . to discard

7. to raise to higher position . . . . apparatus used to transport people between floors in buildings

8. dirt . . . . . fox's home

9. small mammal . . . used in games

10. spring on one foot . . . plant used for brewing beers

11. beloved . . . . expensive

12. rounded mass of earth . . . protuberance on back

13. vertical stake . . . . place where soldier patrols

14. speak falsely . . . have body in horizontal position

15. impress pattern on metal or wood . . . . . bring one's foot down heavily

16. keep safe   jam

17. window shade . . . . . unable to see

18. wooden rod . . . . . glue

19. firmly fixed . . . . . . building to house horses

20. log of wood . . . . . bar the way

 8–10 AVERAGE
11–13 GOOD
14–16 VERY GOOD
17–20 EXCEPTIONAL

Each correct answer scores one point

Part VIII is a series of twenty questions designed to test your ability at innovation. You are given the first part of the word or phrase, and you have to find the second part. The same second part then becomes the first part of a second word or phrase. The dots represent the number of letters in the missing word. Fill in the missing word.

You have twenty minutes to complete the twenty questions.

Double-Words

Example: house . . . . all

Answer: hold.

1. foreign . . . . barrier

2. battle . . . . . suit

3. white . . . . bells

4. stormy . . . . forecast

5. sweet . . . . . throb

6. stair . . . . . . sweeper

7. rocking . . . . . play

8. sheep . . . biscuit

9. brass . . . . stand

10. writing . . . . . towel

11. front . . . step

12. rattle . . . . . bite

13. chariot . . . . track

14. roast . . . steak

15. red . . . . cellar

16. church . . . . . recital

17. puff . . . . . . case

18. boiled . . . cup

19. pearl . . . . . . board

20. cabbage . . . . wings

8–10 AVERAGE
11–13 GOOD
14–16 VERY GOOD
17–20 EXCEPTIONAL

Each correct answer scores one point

TEST FOUR • PART IX

Part IX is a series of ten culture-free tests designed to test your powers of logical reasoning, and understanding of relationships, pattern and design. Study each display of diagrams and select the missing item from the choices given. Study the instructions given to each question.

You have twenty minutes to complete the ten questions.

Example: Ƹ is to / / / /

as () is to ++ , /// , ∞ . =

Answer: = has the same relationship to ()

as / / / / has to Ƹ .

I.

1	2	9
2	4	8
6	6	5

is to

4	4	5
5	6	4
9	8	1

as

3	7	8
4	2	7
1	1	6

is to:

A

6	4	9
7	3	4
4	2	3

B

6	3	4
7	4	9
4	2	3

C

6	9	4
7	4	3
4	3	2

D

6	2	4
7	4	9
4	3	3

2.

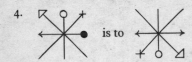

as

3. PUZZLE is to 9∩ZZ⅃Ǝ

as ANSWER is to:

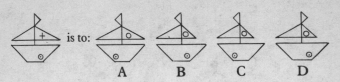

      A   **B**   **C**   **D**

4.

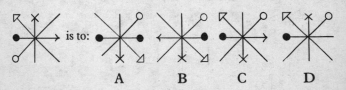

5.

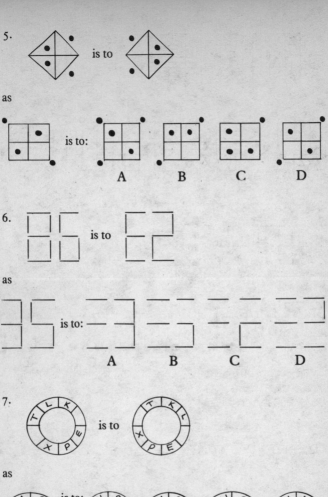

as

A   B   C   D

6.

is to

as

A   B   C   D

7.

is to

as

is to: A   B   C   D

8.

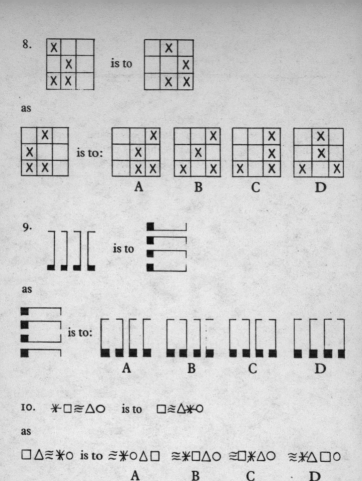

9.

as

10. ✳□≈△○ is to □≈△✳○

as

□△≈✳○ is to ≈✳○△□   ≈✳□△○   ≈□✳△○   ≈✳△□○
                A   B   C   D

8–10   AVERAGE
12–14 GOOD
16   VERY GOOD
18–20 EXCEPTIONAL

Each correct answer scores two points

Part X is a series of ten tests designed to test your powers of calculation and logic. From the alternatives given in each question choose the answer which you think is correct.

You have twenty minutes in which to solve the ten questions.

Calculation and Logic

Example: My watch shows the time at 12.25; one clock shows 12.10. The radio announces 12.30, the church clock strikes 12.00, and your watch shows 12.15. The correct time is 12.20. What is the average time, fast or slow, as shown by these time-pieces?

A. 2 min slow   B. 4 min slow   C. 6 min slow
D. 2 min fast   E. 4 min fast   F. 6 min fast

Answer: B. 4 min slow.

1. If you wrote down all the numbers from 1–100, how many times would you write 3?

   A. 18   B. 19   C. 20   D. 21
   E. 22

2. If seven maids with seven mops cleaned seven floors in seven hours, how long would it take three maids with three mops to clean three floors?

   A. 1 hr   B. 3 hrs   C. 5 hrs
   D. 7 hrs   E. 9 hrs

3. If 12 = 10 and 32 = 26, what does 22 equal?

   A. 16   B. 17   C. 18   D. 19
   E. 20

4. On a pair of eight-faced dice, how many ways can you score six?

   A. 5   B. 6   C. 7   D. 8
   E. 9

5. Town B is 120 miles from Town A. A car travels from A to B at 40 m.p.h. and returns at 30 m.p.h. What was the average speed?

A. 33.6 m.p.h.   B. 34.3 m.p.h.   C. 35.0 m.p.h
D. 35.7 m.p.h.   E. 36.4 m.p.h.

6. What are the chances of scoring over nine with one throw of two dice?

A. 3/36   B. 4/36   C. 5/36
D. 6/36   E. 7/36

7. One man digs a trench in three days; one man digs a trench in five days; one man digs a trench in six days. If they all work together at their same rates as before, how long will they take to dig the trench?

A. 1.2 days   B. 1.4 days   C. 1.6 days
D. 1.8 days   E. 2.0 days

8. How many tennis balls are needed to make up a 4-tier 3-sided pyramid?

A. 19   B. 20   C. 21   D. 22
E. 23

9. Inside a hat is a black or white counter. A white counter is placed in the hat. A white counter is then taken out of the hat. What are the odds against the counter left in the hat being white?

A. 3–1 on   B. 2–1 on   C. evens
D. 2–1 against   E. 3–1 against

10. A rubber ball always bounces up to a height exactly half the height from which it falls. If dropped from 1 metre, how far will the ball travel before coming to rest?

A. 2.4 m   B. 2.6 m   C. 2.8 m
D. 3.0 m   E. 3.2 m

| 8–10 | AVERAGE | 16 | VERY GOOD |
| 12–14 | GOOD | 18–20 | EXCEPTIONAL |

Each correct answer scores two points

TEST FOUR • ANSWERS

TEST FOUR • PART I
1. run 2. rugby (the ball) 3. sea 4. queen
5. paintbrush 6. denim 7. cube 8. wind 9. onion
10. kangaroo 11. nylon 12. tulip 13. stool
14. recuperation 15. bronze 16. sextant 17. guillotine
18. carronade 19. pine 20. catenary

TEST FOUR • PART II
1. compress 2. dwarf 3. confident 4. slenderness
5. harmonious 6. smear 7. burdensome 8. tempt
9. pleasant 10. announcer 11. piece 12. intangible
13. primitive 14. persevering 15. yawning
16. kettledrum 17. medley 18. inform 19. arrange
20. deny

TEST FOUR • PART III
1. expose 2. diverse 3. loth 4. mean 5. order
6. increase 7. elude 8. obedient 9. welcome
10. sluggish 11. ignorant 12. dawn 13. poverty
14. sacred 15. cramped 16. obscure 17. benign
18. smooth 19. unconvincing 20. foreign

TEST FOUR • PART IV
1. window 2. ship 3. pallid 4. bull 5. gallery
6. Oregon 7. eyes 8. peace 9. troupe 10. sponge
11. innoculate 12. family 13. battlefield 14. fortune
15. stranglehold 16. punishment 17. marsupial
18. fawner 19. yellowish 20. secret

TEST FOUR • PART V
1. ludicrous, absurd 2. turbulent,
tumultuous 3. compulsion, duress 4. ecstasy,
rapture 5. tranquil, sedate 6. notable,
remarkable 7. descant, melody 8. complicated,
involuted 9. tilth, cultivation 10. petulant,

irritable 11. swerve, dodge 12. macerate,
steep 13. broach, suggest 14. harbinger,
forerunner 15. listless, languid 16. rummage,
search 17. writhe, squirm 18. glossal,
lingual 19. becket, hook 20. counter, parry

TEST FOUR • PART VI
1. knowing, innocent 2. modification, retention 3. imbue,
clear 4. insolent, polite 5. obtrude, retire 6. endorse,
repudiate 7. jade, enthuse 8. fibre, debility 9. fallacy,
truth 10. craft, honesty 11. export,
consume 12. martial, peaceful 13. modern,
past 14. abdicate, occupy 15. defence,
exposure 16. canvass, pass 17. prosaic, poetic 18. tart,
suave 19. stagnant, brisk 20. whet, nauseate

TEST FOUR • PART VII
1. rose 2. frog 3. ball 4. stock 5. grave 6. shed
7. lift 8. earth 9. bat 10. hop 11. dear 12. hump
13. post 14. lie 15. stamp 16. preserve 17. blind
18. stick 19. stable 20. block

TEST FOUR • PART VIII
1. language 2. dress 3. wedding 4. weather 5. heart
6. carpet 7. horse 8. dog 9. band 10. paper
11. door 12. snake 13. race 14. beef 15. wine
16. organ 17. pastry 18. egg 19. diving 20. butterfly

TEST FOUR • PART IX
1. C 2. C 3. A 4. A 5. D 6. D 7. A 8. A 9. C 10. D

TEST FOUR • PART X
1. C 20 2. D. 7 hrs 3. C. 18 4. A. 5 5. B. 34·3 m.p.h.
6. D. 6/36 7. B. 1.4 days 8. B. 20 9. B. 2–1 on 10. D. 3·0 m

TOTAL SCORE

80–100 AVERAGE	131–160 VERY GOOD
101–130 GOOD	161–200 EXCEPTIONAL

WHAT IS MENSA?

Mensa is a society where the sole qualification for membership is to have attained a score in any supervised test of general intelligence which puts the applicant in the top 2 per cent of the general population.

Founded in 1946 in Oxford, England, Mensa has grown into the international organisation which it is today with some 80,000 members worldwide. The name 'Mensa' is Latin for 'table', indicating a round table society which aims to include intelligent people of every opinion and calling, where no one member, or group of members, has special preference; in fact, all its members are of equal standing within the society.

Mensa is perhaps best described as a social club, where members may communicate with other members through correspondence, meetings, think-ins, dinners, special interest groups, magazines, lectures and international gatherings, and it also provides members with the opportunity to exchange, and try out, new ideas and opinions.

Because it is a round table society Mensa itself has no collective views although, of course, its members do have, and express a very wide array of individual views. Accordingly no one can have the right to speak for Mensa and any views put forward, including those in this book, are of individual members and not Mensa as a whole. The aims of Mensa are quite simply: social and intellectual contact between people world-wide; research into the opinions and attitudes of intelligent people; and the identification and fostering of human intelligence for the benefit of humanity.

If you have enjoyed the tests in this book and have scored reasonably well, why not take the first step towards attaining Mensa membership by writing to one of the addresses listed at the front of the book? If you are successful we hope that membership of the society will bring you the immense amount of pleasure and interest which it has brought to us.